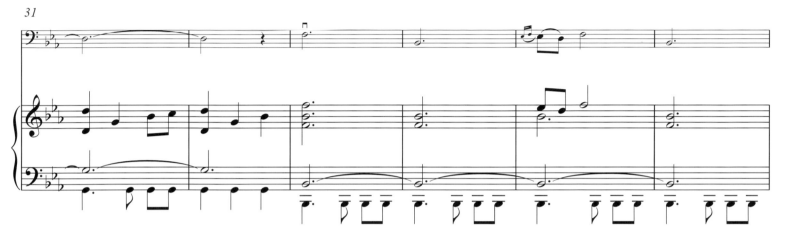

*optional 8va to m. 55

70

76

82

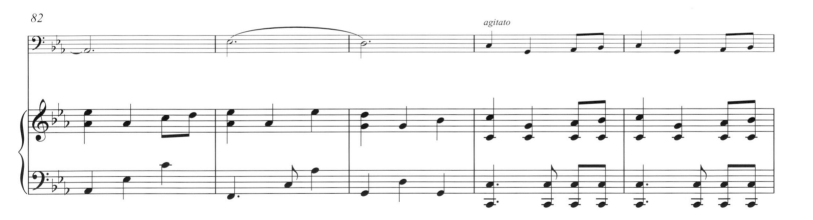

87

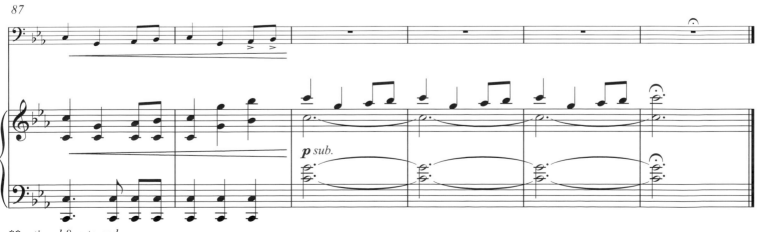

agitato

p sub.

**optional 8va to end*

GAME OF THRONES
Theme from the HBO Series

By RAMIN DJAWADI

CELLO

*optional 8va to m. 55
**optional 8va to end

Also available:

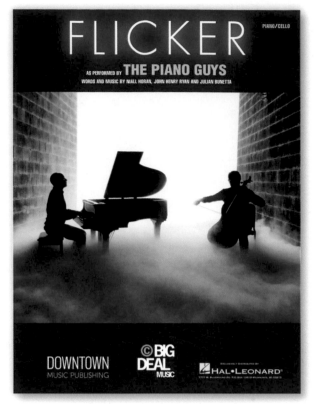

FLICKER – arr. The Piano Guys
Piano/Optional Cello   00263678 $5.99

REWRITE THE STARS – arr. The Piano Guys
Piano/Cello/Violin   00276221 $5.99

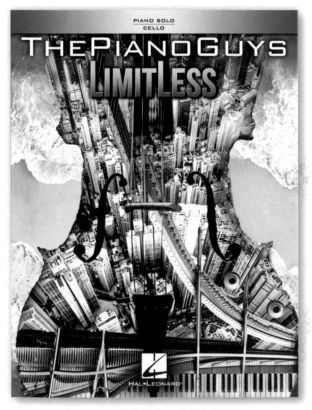

THE PIANO GUYS – LIMITLESS
Piano/Optional Cello   00287509 $19.99

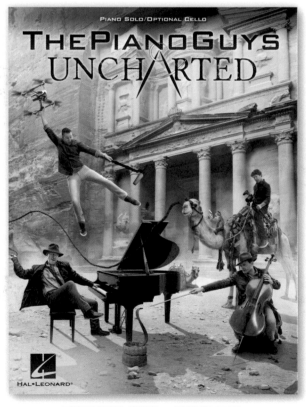

THE PIANO GUYS – UNCHARTED
Piano/Optional Cello   00192941 $19.99